ALACAHÖYÜK

by

Hâmit Zübeyr KOŞAY

Curator of the Ethnografic Museum of Ankara

TURKISH PRESS, BROADCASTING
AND TOURIST DEPARTMENT

PREFACE

Alacahöyük, which contains various different layers of culture and civilisation, dating from 4000 B. C. up to the present day, is a very important excavation site. This site could be compared with Troy, near Çanakkale at Hisarlık, with Alişar, to the northeast of Yozgat, with Yümüktepe near Mersin, and with Açana and Tel-el-Cudeyde near Hatay, in the sense that all these excavations throw light on the prehistoric era. But whereas other important sites enlighten us on various different ages, in Alacahöyük we find represented all the civilizations in Asia Minor, from the Calcholithic age onwards.

The treasures found at Alacahöyük are as rich as those found in Ur (the Sumerian tombs in Mesopotamia), Troy II, Maykop in the Caucasus, and the offerings to the dead· found in the tombs in Mycene in Greece.

Although no archives with cuneiform writings have been found in Alacahöyük such as those in the capital of the Hittites, Boğazkale (Hattusas), or in the trading colony of the Assyrians, Kültepe (Kanesh), it is likely that archives of this sort may yet be discovered, since the excavations so far carried out are by no means very extensive. Both Alacahöyük and the Hittite capital of Boğazkale which is situated thirty kilometres away to the north are and will be very important tourist centres, both for scholars and students of

history, as well as for others interested in these remains.

At present there is a small local museum and excavation hut at Alacahöyük. The excavations were
started in 1935 on behalf of the Turkish Historical Association (Türk Tarih Kurumu) and were continued
in varying degrees of extent up till 1948. The excavators were concerned with Pazarlı (Phrygian), about
thirty kilometres east of the mound, and with the Büyük
Göllücek (Calcholithic) excavations about fifteen kilometres to the south, and in Kalinkaya they opened
one of the tumuli and carefully studied the archaeological possibilities of the district. Although Pazarlı and
Göllücek are not suitable places for visits by large
groups of people, they are, nevertheless, of special in-
terest to archaeologists and well worth a visit by them.

HISTORICAL SURVEY

Since there are known to be places in Anatolia where Stone Age settlements have been discovered, showing that there were human beings living here hundreds of thousands, even millions of years ago, it is possible and indeed very likely that such remains from these very early settlements would be found at the mound (höyük) or in its immediate vicinity. There is no doubt too that when the excavations are completed the existence of remains from the New Stone Age (yeni taş devri) will be established on the sites of the older settlements. The implements and works of art now found at the lower levels of the Alişarhöyük, Pazarlı and Büyük Göllücek excavations belong to the Calcholithic age, which is the age of transition between the polished stone age and the old bronze age.

If we take the year 3500 B. C. and the era following it as a starting point, the picture of human development in the Near and Middle East is as follows. Mesopotamia was still following the cultural trend of the Elubeyds who preceded the Sumerians. While in Anatolia the artisans were still making earthen jars and pots with their hands, there the artisans had already started to use revolving stones for this purpose. In the land of the Elams they were living in the age of Susa I, and were illustrating their pots and pans with stylish animal pictures. The first dynasty hadn't yet started in Egypt and the period of Nagada I was still continuing. It is possible that all these ages correspond to the period of Anau I in Turkestan. It is highly likely that Troy I of Hisarlık and the lowest layer of Alişar are also contemporaries of this age. Finally in Alacahöyük we have the first settlers starting to settle.

In the year 3350 B. C. and the years following it the Uruk culture had come to an end, and from what is shown by the excavation layers we see that the Cemdet Nasir culture, which is as old as the Uruk III period, had begun. At this time it was the fashion to use small tiles for building. In 3200 B.C. the Samis emigrated for the first time to Babel. At the same time in Elam the age of Susa II had commenced. In central Asia the greatest conquerors in world history were now in motion. In Egypt the first dynasty had been established and Menes and his successors had joined together Upper and Lower Egypt. At Abydos the great royal tombs were built, and this, too, was the period of Alacahöyük IV and Troy I. At that time Central Europe was still living in the period of polished stone.

By 2750 B.C. and the years following, the Cemdet Nasir period in Mesopotamia had come to an end and had been succeeded by the Erhanedan period of the Sumerians, and towards 2700 the Sami, although showing traces of Sumerian influence, had also begun to show signs of a culture of their own, and one which was peculiar to themselves. From about this time history starts to be enlightened by written documents. Turning to Egypt we see the fourth dynasty in progress, and in Crete the Minoan age, whereas in Anatolia the periods of Troy II, Alacahöyük III (the age of copper generally known as the Old Bronze Age) and Alişar I are in force.

It is to the years following 2550 that the famous royal tombs of Ur in Sumer belong, and at this same period a very flourishing and brilliant culture was in progress in Alacahöyük. The royal tombs of Alaca date approximately from between the years 2500-2300 B.C. (Alişar Ib) and the most ancient historical documents concerning East and Central Anatolia start with the Akkad Empire in Mesopotamia (which belonged approximately to the twenty-sixth century B.C.). These sources tell us about the military expeditions of the Akkad King Sargon and Naram Sin and also how they brought to their country fruits, trees, silver and precious stones.

The important texts which help historical research concerning central and eastern Anatolia in the beginning of the period from 2000 B.C. are to be found in the cuneiform tablets of Kültepe, Alişar, Boğazköy, Nuzi (Kerkuk) and Assyria. Ancient Anatolia was divided into small provinces ruled by overlords, but it was also possible for these provinces to be ruled by women. By this time Assyrian trading colonies had settled at Kültepe (Kanesh[1].)

·The ancient Hittite Empire was formed in about 1700 B.C. We know one of its rulers was named Anita, that his father's name was Pithana and that their capital was at Kushsara. Shaɾrupkin (Sargon), who at-

---

[1] The trading stations were called "karum". There were "karums" at Uahshushana not far from Kanesh, at Purushan, some three days journey away, and in the north at Hurana and Durhumi near Boğazköy. Besides the "karums" there were secondary stations called Uabartum (alien dwellings). A great many karums were closely related to Kanesh, and Kanesh in turn was linked with Assyria. Pins, combs and tin were imported from the East, and in the internal trade copper, silver and gold articles had a very important role. Large corporations were established in order to keep trade running smoothly.

tempted to conquer Northern Anatolia, lived about the
same time as Pithana, however on a tablet found in
Alişar it is his son Anita's name that is mentioned,
and it was Anita who joined all the towns, including
Boğazköy (Hattusash), under his rule[1].

Of his successors, Lebarnas, who remains one of
the greatest founders of the Hittite Empire, brought
the capital to Boğazköy and extended the boundaries
of the country to the Black Sea in the north and to the
Mediterranean in the south[2].

---

[1] It is very likely that the first overlords were the
Proto-Hittites. In the Proto-Hittite language the relative suffix
is "il" and the feminine suffix is "an", e.g. Hattuş-il Kattah.
Besides this there is a principal language in Anatolia which
for the present is called the "✕" language, and the place
names which end with "anda" and "assha" belong to this
period. This language stretches from Greece to Syria, and
was also used by the Kizuatna and the Arzanas. During the
time of the Hittites it is possible to differentiate between the
following groups in Anatolia: the Hatti (Proto-Hittite), Lui
and Pala.

[2]   The Hittite State in Central Anatolia is divided into
two periods, consisting of the old empire (1950-1475) and
the new empire (1475-1192). These two periods, again, are
studied according to various dynasties:

The Kussar Dynasty: (1950-1650)
The Hattusas I Dynasty: (1650-1550) The Old Empire
The Hattusas II Dynasty: (1550-1475)
The Hattusas III Dynasty: (1475-1192) The New Em-
                                                            pire

The most important kings of the Kussar dynasty were:
Pithana, Anita, Tuthalias I (the contemporary of Hamura-
bi of Babel), (1800-1757), Pusaruma, Povalitelmah, Lebarnas, and Hattusilis I. The most important kings of the
Hattusas dynasty were: Mursilis I, (who conquered Babel in
1600), Hantilis I, Zidantas I, and Ammunas. The most important kings of the Hattusas II dynasty were: Huzziyas I,
Telepinus, Alluvandas, Hantilis II, Zidantas II, Huzziyas II.

His son Hattusilis I besieged Syria and after his death Mursilis I first captured Aleppo and then led an expedition to Mesopotamia in the year 1600 and destroyed Babel. He was finally killed by his brother-in-law Hantilis. In the time of Hantilis the Kashkas for the first time attacked from the North East. Boğazköy was fortified, but after the king's death civil war broke out and the country suffered from starvation, drought and plague. The state of anarchy was at last ended by Telepinus, and in the year 1450 B.C. the era of the new Hittite state commenced. Of this period the most famous kings were: Shubbiluliuma, Mursilis II and Hattushil III. The chief historical events of the age can be summarised as follows: Shubbiluliuma was a contemporary of the Egyptian king Ikhnaton. Shubbiluliuma attacked Syria, and having defeated the king of the Mittanis, Tushratta, conquered the capital of Vashukanni and reduced it to ruins. Thus the Hittite state and that of the Egyptians became neighbours and there now commenced the great struggle which was to last for five years. The Hittite king nominated his sons as governors of Kargamish and Aleppo, and annexed the Mittani state to his own as a colony thereof. The widow of Ikhnaton wished to marry one of the sons of Shubbiluliuma, but whilst he was on his way to her country the bridegroom was murdered. Thereupon ci-

---

The most important kings of the dynasty of Hattusas III were: Tuthalias II, Hattusilis II, Tuthalias III, Arnuvandas I, Shubbiluliuma (his government 1395-1315). Arnuvandas 1353 II, Mursilis II (1353-1315), Muvattalis (1315-1290), Urhtesup (1290-1283), Hattusilis III (1283-1250), Tuthalias IV (1250-1220), Arnuvandas III (1220-1205), Tuthalias V (1205-1192). Some reliefs of these kings were found in the Temple of Yazılıkaya at Boğazkale.

vil war broke out in the land of the Hitittes and Arnuvandas II, the son of Shubbiluliuma, was unable to
bring about peace. The Empire was saved from complete dismemberment by his younger brother Mursilis
II, who waged systematic war on the Kashkas and conquered Arzava. His son Muvattalis again came in con-
tact with the Egyptians, and in the year 1288 B. C. the
battle of Kadeşh resulted in favour of the Hittites. At
this time Rameses II was reigning in Egypt. However
the Assyrians, taking advantage of these battles, conquered some sections of the land of the Mittanis. Urbi
Tesnup, the son of Muvattalis, left his throne to his
uncle Hattusilis III, and a peace treaty was signed
with Egypt in the year 1272 B.C. Meanwhile however,
since the Assyrians and the Hittites were neighbours,
their relations grew progressively more difficult.

In the time of Tuthalias IV there commenced the
Aegean immigration which was to prepare the downfall of the Hittite state, and during the reign of King
Arnuvandas III the threat from the west and north-
west also increased. Finally, in the time of Tuthalias
V, a new immigration pushed the Hittites out of Anatolia altogether and they were left to establish small
governorships in the Taurus and Antitauros mountains and in the surrounding districts. Meanwhile the
Phrygians flourished in what was left of the Hittite
state.

The Phrygians:

Before this tribe reached Anatolia the Mushkis,
who are supposed to be closely related to the Phrygians, are known to have established some provinces in
central Anatolia, having arrived thither from the east.
The Assyrians speak of them as **Muscia.** Under the

reign of five kings these occupied a certain section of Assyrian country. Tiglath-Pileser I (1115-1095 B.C.), tells of how he conquered them, and later Tukulti Ninurta II (890-885 B.C.) also speaks of the victories he had gained over the Mushkis.

In 718 the Mushki king Mita incited the smaller states to rebel against the Assyrians, however the uprisings were pacified by Sargon II (722-709). In 717 Mita formed an alliance with the Urartos and the king of Kargamiş, Pisiris, both of whom were deadly enemies of the Assyrians. Sargon II speaks of how he crossed the Taurus mountains in 715 and 716 and conquered twenty-two towns from the Phrygians. In 712 B.C. Sargon II invaded the territory of the allies and took Gauraina, and in 709 he conquered the entire land of the Mushkis. A few years later we have the first appearance of the Cimmerians in Anatolia. These were the vanguard of the Cimmerians who came in waves from the south of Russia, the Caucasus. Thereupon Argistis, the king of Urarto, broke off the struggle with the Assyrians, but although he managed to drive back the attackers his country naturally suffered as a result of these invasions.

In the year 706 B.C. the Assyrian King Sargon II was killed in battle while fighting against the Cimmerians. The Phrygians also suffered considerable losses, and Lydia regained its complete independence.

During the reign of the Assyrian king Esarhaddon (680-669 B.C.) an attack on an even larger scale was launched by the Cimmerians, they being by this time in alliance with the Medes, and having thus become even more dangerous. Although the Assyrians temporarily repelled this attack with the help of the Scythians in the year 680 B.C. the Phrygian state suffered heavily and its king Midas committed suicide. In 652 B.C. it was the turn of the Lydian state to become the victim of the Cimmerians, and as a result Gyges lost his throne and Sardis was plundered. The Cimmerians later intermingled with the natives and the Scythians, and in course of time the Lydian state was re-established. King Alyattes, in 590 B.C., advancing towards the west met the Median King Astyages and in 585 a treaty was signed between these two kings. Following this, there commenced the great struggle between the Lydians and the Persians. Croesus, the king of the Lydians, became the prisoner of the Perisan king Cyrus and Sardis was occupied by the Persians. After this Anatolia enjoyed two centuries of peace under the Achaemenes. At this time Anatolia was divided up into satrapies and after the downfall of the Persian Empire these satrapies were preserved by Alexander the Great. However after the sudden death of Alexander the Great at Babel (323 B.C.) Anatolia became once again the scene of war. There can be very little doubt that Alacahöyük, which was a place of some importance and culture, near Boğazkale, must have been considerably influenced by all these historical events and that it played its part in the developments which took place.

Cultural Age	Layers		Buildings	Comparison with Boğazköy	Date.
I.	1	Roman, Byzantine, Selçuk Ottoman Villages. Phrygians.		II.	The brilliant Age of the Phrygians.
	2	The Great Empire of the Hittites.	Door with the Sphinx, great temple, earth ramparts, walls	III b.	1300 B. C.
II.	3 a/b	The settlement of the first Hittites.	Second temple.	III a.	1400 B. C.
			Hierogliph, marks, pots, stone walls.	IV.	1700—1400 B. C.
	4	Remnants of the Cappadocians.	Walls made of small walls.	Kültepe V.	2000 B.C.
III.	5	Copper Age	Royal tombs (approximate date 2500 - 2300 B. C.)	------	3000 B. C.
	1		Brick houses with stone foundations.		
	8				
IV.	9 1 14	Calcholithic	Stone foundations and brick houses.	------	3500—3000 B. C.

How to Get to Alacahöyük.

Since any person who pays many visits either to Alacahöyük or to Boğazköy is certain to visit the other also, we need to take both these sites of excavation into consideration when answering the above question.

1. Those who visit Boğazkale[1] travel by train as far as Çerikli, and from thence go by bus to Sungurlu where they can hire a horse carriage to take them to Boğazköy. Since Çerikli is a small station it is impossible to find hotel accommodation there, and at times when transport is overcrowded it may sometimes happen that places are very difficult to find. However in Sungurlu there is a municipal inn and a hotel converted from a private house, and with the help of the proprietor of this hotel it is possible to procure the horse carriages. If, however, any difficulties should arise here it is advisable to get in touch with the governor, or alternatively with the municipality or the education officer. It is only by chance that one can find a motor car or taxi in Sugurlu. If one makes the tour of the "kale" (castle) and Yazılıkaya in Boğazkale by car it is possible to finish it in one day and return to Sungurlu in the evening; but if one is making the tour on foot then it is necessary to spend a night at Boğazkale. Although there are no hotels here one can, with the help of the director of the district, stay as a guest in one of the private houses. After having seen Boğazkale one can proceed in one's horse carriage to Alacahöyük, which lies some thirty kilomet-

---

[1] The official name for Boğazköy is now Boğazkale and it is an administrative centre.

res to the north of it. It is indeed advisable to go by carriage as the road is extremely bad, and if one does travel by car it is advisable to find out whether the driver knows the way, failing which it is necessary to have a guide.

2. During the summer months it is possible to reach Boğazkale by car by the Bala, Keskin, Çerikli and Sungurlu roads, and there are quite a number of people who do this.

3. One can also travel to Boğazköy via Yozgat. After reaching Yerköy by train one can go on to Yozgat by the municipality bus, and here there is quite a good municipality hotel, as well as another private hotel and inns. In the summer season too it is possible to reach Boğazkale by taxi via the mountain road to the north west of Yozgat. This is, however, a difficult road, and the tourist road between Yozgat and Boğazkale has not yet been completed.

4. If one wants to visit Alacahöyük first it is possible to book seats on the small buses working between Ankara and Samsun and to get off at Alaca. Ankara - Alaca tickets are approximately twelve liras, but this does not include heavy baggage. At Alaca one can hire a horse carriage with the help of the municipality. The distance between Alaca and the Höyük (the Mound) is about fifteen kilometres, and those tourists travelling in parties can hire the municipality bus to make this journey. From the Höyük, travelling in the opposite direction, one can get carriages for conveyance to Boğazköy, and after seeing this site the visitor can then go on by carriage to Sungurlu or Alaca.

If one receives permission from the director of the Alacahöyük Excavations, in the Turkish Historical Association (Türk Tarih Kurumu) in Ankara, one may then stay actually in the excavation house in Höyük which belongs to this Association. For a small fee given to the excavation guard one can procure such eatables as chicken, eggs and rice (pilav), but those travellers who are not accustomed to village pastries are advised to take bread with them from Alaca or Yozgat.

5. Those people who wish to go by private car to Alacahöyük can take advantage of the road from Bala-Kaman, Yerköy, Yozgat and Alaca. Although this is a very long road, being about three hundred and sixty kilometres, it is quite a good one and fairly well frequented. About fifteen kilometres from Kirşehir, at a point beside the Çogun police station, the road turns off to Yerköy, and from the Ciçek mountain on to Yerköy the scenery is extremely beautiful.

As we have mentioned above, the road between Alacahöyük and Boğazköy is rather stony for cars, so that drivers taking this route usually go by a slightly longer way via Kücük-Ekmekci, and Kirankişla to the good road of Sungurlu. However this is a tiring and difficult process and on rainy days the road becomes so muddy that one can only get through by truck or jeep.

6. In order to pay a visit to the Pazarlı and Göllücek excavation sites it is necessary to procure a guide from the Höyük museum guard.

Once the road between Ankara, Kırıkale, and Çerikli has been completed, and that between Sungurlu, Boğazkale and Höyük put into a better state of repair it will be very much easier to visit this area. It would be an excellent idea if the Mayor of Çorum got in touch

with the General Director of the Tourism Department
with a view to building a tourist hotel in Boğazkale or
even to converting a suitable house for this purpose,
and also, within the limits of possibility, in order to
improve the roads in the area.

Historical Account of the Excavations
at Alacahöyük

Proper archaeological researches in Alacahöyük
started in 1935, on behalf of the Turkish Historical
Association, and continued until 1948.

Alacahöyük has been known to the world of archaeology since the middle of the XIXth century. W.G.
Hamilton, in his travels in Anatolia in 1835, paid a visit to the Höyük and saw the door with the Sphinx,
but at this date it was not known that this door belonged originally to the Hittites. The name of Hamilton's
book is "Researches in Asia Minor, Pontus and Armen-
ia" (2 Vols. 1872). Because of its proximity to Kara-
hisar in the north Hamilton calls the Höyük "Karahi-
sar-Euyuk". However the drawings, which he did very
hurriedly, are not accurate. Charles Texier, too, in his
work called "Description de l'Asie Mineure" (Paris
1839) repeats the observations of Hamilton (Vol. I
pp. 223/4).

H. Barth in his travels from Scutari to Trebizond
also stopped at the Höyük and subsequently published
an article in "Denkmäler und Forschungen, No. 126,
juni 1859" under the title of "Über die Ruinen bei Ve-
jük im alten Kappadocien".

In 1861 A.D. Mordmann gave interesting details
about Boğazköy, Höyük and Cappodocia. In 1869
H. G. Von Lennep carried out researches in the Hö-

yük, while a few years earlier, in 1865, G. Perrot had made the first plan of the tower to the left and the right of the door with the Sphinx (Prothyron). Then in 1881 W. Ramsay and Wilson visited the Höyük and uncovered some further reliefs near this same door. The underground way and the second door between the Sphinxes had already been opened in 1863 by Ernest Chantre. With reference to Alaca Chantre called the Höyük "Euyuk d'Aladja".

In 1906 an expedition led by H. Winekler-Makridi, who worked at Boğazkale, decided also to work on the Höyük and in the following year Makridi uncovered the turret to the left of the door with the Sphinx and exposed more clearly the reliefs in front of it.

During the years (1926-1927) the Höyük was also visited by Von der Osten who published his report in the Chicago Oriental Institute.

The first systematic excavations in Alacahöyük, carried out with the science required by archaeology, started in 1935. The first year's excavations were made by Dr. Hamit Koşay and Archaeologist Remzi Oğuz Arik on behalf of the Turkish Historical Association. From 1936 to 1949 the excavations at the Höyük and in the surrounding area were again conducted by Dr. Hamit Koşay in association with other Turkish archaeologists and technicians[1].

---

[1] These include Architect Mazhar, Architect Süleyman Örnek, Abdullah Altar, Archaeologist Hakkı Gültekin, Archaeologist Kadri Erdil, Archaeologist Doçent Bahadır Alkım, Kemal Turfan, Archaeologist Mahmut Akok, Archaeologist Doçent Tahsin Özgüç, Archaeologist Nezih Fıratlı, Archaeologist Raci Temizer, Photographer Baha Bediz, Schüler, Designer Ömer Üçüncü, all of whom took part in the Alacahöyük excavations.

Bibliography

Remzi Oğuz Arık   : *Alacahöyük Hafriyatı 1935* (published 1937).

Remzi Oğuz Arık   : *Les fouilles d'Alacahöyük 1935* (published 1937).

Dr. Hamit Zübeyr Koşay : *Alacahöyük hafriyatı 1936* (published 1938)

„   „   „   : *Augsgrabungen von Alacahöyük 1936* (published 1944).

„   „   „   : *Alacahöyük hafriyatı 1940 çalışmaları* (published 1941, in *Belleten* 17-18.)

„   „   „   : Türk Tarih Kurumu tarafından Alacahöyükte yaptırılan hafriyatta elde edilen neticeler 1937 (Read in the second Congress of the Historical Association of Turkey).

„   „   „   : *A Great Discovery (The Illustrated London News.* July 21, 1945).

„   „   „   : *Alacahöyük* (In English) (published in *La Turquie Kemaliste.* No. 15/1936).

„   „   „   : *Alacahöyük 1937-1939.*

and Mahmut Akok   : *The Pottery of Alacahöyük (American Journal of Archeology* Vol. LI. No. 2/1947)

Dr. H. Z. Koşay - M. Akok : *Alacahöyük 1940-1941* (Ready to be published).

„   „   „   : *Alacahöyük 1942-1948* (in preparation).

Prof. Dr. Şevket Aziz Kansu : *Alacahöyükte bulunan iskeletlerin antropolojik tetkiki. (Belleten* C. I sayı I. 1937).

„   „   „   : *Etude Anthropologique de quelques squelettes d'Alacahöyük. (L'Anthropologie* Paris T. 47. No. 1/2/1937).

Prof. Dr. Ş. A. Kansu-Doç. Dr. Seniha Tunakan : *Alacahöyük kazılarında (1936-1944) Bakır Çağı yerleşme katlarından çıkarılan iskeletlerin antropolojik incelenmesi* (Belleten sayı 36/1945).

Dr. Franz Hancar   : *Alacahöyük Wiener Beiträge zur Kunst und Kultur geschichte (Asiene Band XII/1938).*

„   „   „   : *Alacahöyük Kült Standartlarının tefsirine dair* (Firuzan Kınal çevirmesi. *Belleten* 34/1945).

Helmuth Th. Bossert : *Alt Anatolien* Berlin 1942.

Ekrem Akurgal   : *Spaethethitische Bildkunst.* Ankara 1949.

VISITING THE MUSEUM

The Garden in front of the Museum:

In the middle of the garden there is a statue of a lion which comes from an ancient building. This was brought from the garden of Imamoğlu in front of the door with the Sphinx.

On the east side there is a series of various Hittite works found in the Höyük and in the neighbouring area. One of these, representing a god on a human shoulder, was the first work of art to be brought to the surface in 1935.

The piece which represents a hunting scene, together with the one beside it, was brought from a place called Koşkyeri, near the Höyük vineyards. It has been discovered that these were originally taken from the Höyük to be used in a Byzantine church.

On the lefthand side there is a series of stone works belonging to the Roman and Byzantine period. There are also sacrificial stones and tombstones inscribed in Greek.

In the open area beside the stairs one sees square baths belonging to the Hittite age, and also big provision jugs.

The Interior of the Museum:

The exhibits are divided up according to chronology and types:

A: **Calcholithic, or copper-stone** age (3500-3000 B.C.).

On the righthand side of the entrance exhibits from Alacahöyük and Büyük Göllücek can be seen.

The distinctive qualities of this age are as follows:

Copper tools are very rare. In the excavation at Büyük Göllücek, although many thousands of earthenware objects were found, the number of metal articles found here does not exceed four. Utility articles are mostly made of stone, flint, obsidien, and of bone. Since woodwork, cloth and leatherwork has been destroyed by time it is very difficult to give any opinion on these. However pots and pans, which preserve their original ingredients and quality, are of very great importance. There are no written documents concerning this period with the exception of certain signs or seals. Human beings of this period possessed a widely developed system of agriculture and animal husbandry which they had inherited from the Neolithic age. The different types of pots and pans and their forms, and especially some of the decorated pieces, leave no doubt that there was a marked development in the field of art.

Pots and Pans:

Ninety-five percent of these are of very crude work. They are practically all made by hand, their ingredients having been mixed with an addition of sand or straw. The surfaces were given a coat of paint before baking, and some of them were given a second special coat later. These paint coatings took on different colours, such as black, red, and shades of yellow, according to the smoky quality or otherwise of the fire on which they were baked.

Among the objects not intended for daily use there are some very delicate and refined specimens. It is probable that the mud which was used for these was very carefully sieved and prepared, and in very rare pieces the aesthetic effect has been increased by the addition of decorations in red and white paint over the final coating. With regard to the handles, with very few exceptions these are made in a somewhat amateurish style and very close to the body of the pot. The pots are finished off with finely tapered edges. Pans in the shape of fruit dishes, wide-mouthed pots, and jugs are special features of this age.

One can see how during the Calcholithic age the artisan who made pots and pans, although in many ways following the traditional forms of construction, was, at the same time, struggling to find new ones.

When one turns the corner one sees a tomb belonging to the Calcholithic age. The skeleton was brought here just as it was found, together with all the accompanying paraphanalia that surrounded it. It was buried with the knees of the corpse bent.

B: The Old Bronze Age, (3000-2000 B.C.).

This is generally referred to as the Copper age. In the glass cases one can see the valuable specimens found in the tombs of the kings, who were extremely rich. These objects were all taken from the fifth to eighth layer of building, before that of the Hittites. They belong approximately to the period round about 2500 B.C. and consist of various weapons, and crowns known as "diadems" etc. On the walls one can see enlarged photographs and drawings denoting exactly how and where they were found.

In the middle of the room, in a big jug, one can see one of the poor tombs of this age. In this too the skeleton was found with the knees bent, (Hocher),

In the case opposite, the pots and pans of the Copper age and the small findings belonging to that age are exhibited. The burnt cereals are also remnants of this period.

The pots and pans, with very few exceptions, are of one colour. But delicacy and richness of form meet the eye right from its very first glance. Painted coatings are very much in evidence during this period. If one leaves aside the coarse kitchen ware there are quite a number of dinner and wine sets which denote a rich life.

The line decorations of the Calcholithic age are more advanced and have been developed into deep gratings and reliefs. If there are any lines these are often filled in with a white material, and black, red, brown and multicoloured paint coatings are very carefully recoated with a further layer.

The metal dishes made during this period (gold, copper, silver and bronze) in form resemble the earthenware specimens. From this it can be deduced that generally speaking the metal dishes were also local products.

In this age too we continue to find flints, knives and bone instruments being made, but it is impossible to obtain any information concerning the woodwork and needlework of the time.

C. The Hittite Age: (2000-1200 B.C.).

If one examines the cases one after another one will notice that they are divided up under the headings of old, middle and new. This division has been made according to architectural levels and does not necessarily refer to political levels or periods. The middle architectural level is very likely connected with the old Hittite state.

The age which is known as the Copper age, and which is approximately about the third millenium, ended with a most disastrous fire. Invasions, together with the migration of various tribes to this area, gave rise to an age which is known in general as the Hittite age, and which possessed a distinctive new culture. Nor is it necessary that all the tribes in this new cultural area should have been Hittite. The old influences were not entirely swept away, but were modified by the new cultural trends which set the seal of their own character upon them.

The unicoloured pots and pans are once again predominant during this period, but at the same time one finds pieces decorated with red and brown lines and bands over a white background. The pots and pans were made on a revolving wheel and before being baked they were carefully coated with paint, which was very carefully smoothed over so as to guard against the leakage of water. Sometimes however the coating of paint was not so carefully put on and the pot was simply dipped in it.

Amongst the Hittite pots and pans there is a great variety of different shapes and sizes. There are big pots, small pots, triangular plates with handles, deep plates with no handles, water jugs with handles (like those in Troy), very beautiful water jugs with legs and various other coloured items of this kind. Amongst these the most typical of this period are those jugs with mouths fashioned in the shape of a bird's head or beak. It has been concluded from various reliefs that these decorated water jugs were used in religious ceremonies.

The square bath-tubs, accompanied by little stools for sitting on, show that the Hittites were in the habit of washing frequently.

In the Hittite kitchens one finds dishes shaped like bunches of grapes, tripods in the shape of animals' legs, drinking glasses in the shape of bulls or heads of birds, and sieves and lids for dishes. In one species of Hittite cooking dish a charcoal burner was constructed in such a way as to be attached to the dish (an example of this type is to be found in the Ankara Museum). Amongst the Hittite dishes there are some which, to our eyes, appear oddly shaped. For example, quite a number of them have pointed bottoms. But if we study carefully the way of life of this period it is quite natural that that should be so, for these dishes were kept in the kitchen by burying the points in the earth. The smaller dishes, in order that they should not topple over, were placed into round circles of baked earth.

In general we can accept the fact that the forms of the pots and pans in central Asia Minor excercised an influence on Troy and the western islands, and were at the same time influenced in their turn by the style pertaining to these areas.

In this age too we find a continuation of the age of polished stone, which also excercised a considerable influence over the Hittites. Among the Hittites, as a legacy of this former age, we find instruments made of flint. Work on bone has risen to a high stage of art, and amongst the metal instruments bronze is predominant. Although iron was known it was very rarely used. As in all ages gold and silver was used in the making of decorative objects and also for pots and pans.

One of the glass cases of the Museum is devoted to copper objects, most of which contain a high degree of iron. These articles were made at the Höyük itself, and this is proved by the fact that a great deal of the same material was found in the smelting works to the west of the great temple. The iron was brought from some distance away. Nowadays one can still find copper in the Lafa village of the Iskilip district, in the area belonging to Mehmet Ilgaz Yunus.

In the glass case in the centre are exhibited the smaller finds. On the walls hang comparative charts showing the various sites of excavation for Hittite remains, together with other charts concerning the chronology of the Hittites according to various different scholars. Besides these there are collections which help to facilitate the comparison between different types of handle as well as other pieces which are helpful for the purposes of comparison. On the wall opposite the door there is a relief plan of the Höyük[1].

D: The Phrygian Age (1200-600 B.C.).

The Phrygian works found at Alacahöyük and at

[1] In the last excavation layer of the Copper age (Layer V) and the first layer belonging to the Hittites pots and pans have been found belonging to the type known as Cappadocian. It has not yet been possible to relate it to any one architectural level, but these articles which having been compared with those found in Alişar are dated from the Old Bronze age were especially found in Kültepe. They belong to a short while before the period of the Assyrian trade colonies.

Pazarlı in the same period are displayed in the Museum in two different glass cases. In the Phrygian age one finds extremely decorative specimens of pottery, with red or brown lines on a white background, and at the same time there are other examples coloured in black or red, though the latter type is the more predominant. Although it is quite evident that here a new movement in art is in progress in the place of the old Hittite art, yet these are not entirely new but are based upon the old legacies and traditions of the arts which have gone before them. The multicoloured pieces of pottery with their geological designs almost remind one of the rebirth of the old tradition of Asia Minor, while the uncoloured ones recall the spreading of the old Anatolian tradition. At last, in this period, metal work starts to show its influence on the earthenware and the artisan began to attempt on earthenware the bold shapes hitherto used on metal only. Amongst the decorative designs of this period different styles begin to take shape and human representations as well as those of animals and flowers are very much in evidence. In the Phrygian age too ironware objects became more common though at the same time stone and bone works continued.

In a different case are displayed objects belonging to different periods which were found in the district of Çorum and were presented to the Museum by the Educational Director of Çorum. Amongst them is a rython drinking vessel belonging to the Phrygian age which is especially attractive and worthy of attention.

Ethnographic collection: At Alacahöyük the excavation group gave quite a lot of importance to local ethnographic research. The material collected by Hamit Koşay and the painter Osman Yalçin concerning the ethnographic folklore of Alacahöyük has been presented to the Historical Association of Turkey (Türk Tarih Kurumu) for publication. Zehra Örnek also collected valuable material, especially with regard to the tapestries and woven material of the district. In one of the cases are displayed specimens of local weaving work and other items of the same nature which have been presented to the museum by the peasants.

In a case near the door are displayed the publications concerning the researches at Alacahöyük[1].

Visiting the Excavation Area

The Walls of the Old Town:

During the Hittite age and even before the Höyük was surrounded by a wall. In order to construct this wall a certain quantity of special earth had to be transported to the spot from some other locality and with this an earthen rampart of about twenty-five to thirty yards wide was raised on which parallel stone walls were built to form a foundation. The gaps between these walls were then filled in, thus forming the second layer of the rampart, and on top of that the wall proper was constructed. The first earthen rampart and the stone walls can still be seen in parts.

Under the city walls it was usual to build secret passages for the soldiers to pass through, which were usually given the name of poteru. One of these secret passages is still visible on the western side of the Höyük; compare with Yerkapı at Boğazkale. The main gate of the city, the gate with the Sphinx is situated to the

---

[1] The publications of the Historical Association of Turkey can be obtained directly from the Ministry of Education publications distributing centre in Ankara.

south. In front of this gate there were two towers
which jutted out in the shape of an elbow, and on the
base of these towers were found reliefs which are now
in the Museum of Ankara. (The bull which represented Teshub and the priestking on a pedestal walking
towards him.)

The Sphinx, which has the body of a lion and the
face of a girl, was supposed to defend the city. Its
headgear, which is now broken, was in the form of a
conical hat. On the righthand side can be seen a Hittite
god who is represented with a long dress, standing on
a two-headed eagle, which holds in his claws a double
rabbit. In the inner niches of the door, on the foot of
a raised statue, there are still some reliefs remaining.
The towers which were connected to the walls are
now destroyed.

Following the excavations of Makridi the Sphinx
on the lefthand side fell down, but the group of excavators from the Historical Association succeeded in put-
ting it back into its original place and also reinforced
the foundations in such a way as to resemble the original setting.

In the area in front of the door with the Sphinx
there are statues of lions and bulls. These are all çarved
according to the Hittite style of art, though on one
of the lions a later addition in the form of Phrygian
inscriptions has been made.

Hittite Temples:

If one looks to the north from the door of the
Sphinx one can see a double door which forms the
entrance to a temple of the new Hittite period. (Age
II, Architectural level 2). Deep excavations have been

made between the temple and the door with the Sphinx and have resulted in the finding of architectural layers 3a and 3b. The layer which stretches up to and underneath the door with the Sphinx gives the impression of another, open, temple, possessing a middle courtyard with rooms clustered round it.

In the great hollow on the western side, under the middle Hittite architectural layers, have been found other layers belonging to the old Hittite age. Since these had to be removed in order to get down to lower levels it was only possible to follow them by taking note of the area over which they spread. The slanting buildings seen on the west side of the hollow belong to the third and fourth architectural layers, and the great building on the earthen mound belongs to the second architectural layer.

As one enters through the gate of the new Hittite age temple one is confronted by a great courtyard, open in the front. This courtyard and the building as a whole have been constructed on a slant, and have been broadened with porticos to the right and left.

The rooms which coincided with the lefthand hole have been removed in order to make it possible to dig down to still deeper layers. The temple was protected from the collapse of the city walls by the talus walls.

The sewerage system in architectural layers 2, 3a and 3b show that the Hittites were very advanced in town planning. The water supplies in different rooms were linked by means of earthen pipes to small channels, and these channels in turn led into a larger channel.

The Phrygians made use of the Hittite buildings, to which they made a number of additions or alterations

(Age I, Architectural layer I). The original level of the ground is shown by the tree in the excavation area. The blockage to the left of this was made to reinforce a big Hittite edifice, but at one point this has been severed and by digging down to a deeper layer the excavators have discovered remains from the Calcholithic age at the original ground level on which the Höyük (mound) was constructed.

The Age known as the Copper age:

Cultural age III: Layer 5-8. In the deep hole thirteen rich tombs, belonging to royal families, have been discovered (dated at approximately 2500 B.C.), all of which were found to be in an excellent state of preservation, and which have given to the Höyük an even greater importance. Since the last layers of the Copper age had been burnt and reduced to ashes and the whole area covered over by ruins, the Hittites were not aware of the existence of the tombs.

Generally speaking the tombs are square in shape, and the corpses inside them were usually buried with their heads pointing towards the west and their feet towards the east. The dead bodies were placed with their knees bent and on their heads there were golden crowns, while by their sides had been placed gold, silver or earthen bowls, sun discs in the shape of crescents, objects of decoration and idols. Of all the tombs, so far the only efforts at preservation have been made on H tomb, at the top, by means of building walls to reinforce it. The tombs were built very close to the houses in which the people were living at the time, indeed it is highly possible that some of the houses were even removed in order to clear a space for the royal tombs.

During this age the custom of burial whereby the body was placed inside a large pot or vessel was also commonly in force. In 1935 the excavators dug down some way below the area beside C tomb and found architectural layers of the 13-9 Calcholithic age and also some skeletons.

Alacahöyük Cultural age IV:

The Calcholithic age:

In 1935 the original earth surface was reached with great difficulty, through water and through the royal tombs of the Copper age. However in the area of the Hittite blockage Calcholithic remains were encountered in a comparatively high layer and on drier land.

When the first inhabitants of the Höyük arrived in this area (between 4000-3000 B.C.), they found a natural hillock at the mouth of the springs here, and on it they formed the nucleus of the Höyük, later extending it to the sloping area which surrounded it. When new towns later came to be formed on top of one another the water seeped into the towns on the lower levels and accumulated therein.

The area round the poteru at the door on the west side of the Höyük was dug and here was found one of the old towers and parts of the city walls. The poteru formed a curve on the inside and in later periods were of considerable benefit, being incorporated into the sewerage system.

In the south west section of the Höyük too, a district was uncovered which proved to be specially rich in respect to the objects which were discovered there.

Although work has been carried on in Alacahöyük to a greater or less degree from 1935 to 1949 yet

the excavation necessary here is by no means completed. If one works over a wide area it is possible to
find Phrygian, Hittite and Calcholithic districts on top
of one another, and it is very likely that a great deal
of very valuable material is still buried here and also
that there is a large archive in the Hittite layer. If the
wide area beside the blockage is more deeply excavated
it will be immensely profitable for the advancement
of our knowledge concerning the Calcholithic age. The
various foundations found above the Phrygian layer
are those of peasants' dwellings - mostly ancestors of
the present dwellers of the Höyük.

When the excavation group of the Historical Association first started work the whole village was inhabited, but this was almost entirely removed, in return
for help and compensation which was given to the vil-
lagers, and only a few houses on the sides of the Höyük were allowed to remain. In order to preserve the
excavation area, however, it is most advisable that
these houses also should be removed as soon as possible.

PAZARLI

Pazarlı is situated 29 kilometres east of Alacahöyük. The route leading to it follows the road to Ala-
ca-Çorum until it reaches the village of Küre, and here one turns eastwards. After having left Küre one pas-
ses through the southern edge of the village of Koyun-
lu and thence through yet another small village, after
which one enters into an area of wooded, bushy country. One comes next to the village of Çıkhasan, and
from here the Phrygian castle of Pazarlı is only about
ten minutes walk distant. The Pazarlı district is cut by
many small streams and rivers and is surrounded by
mountains, having to the north-east the Akdağ mountain chain (approximately one thousand, seven hundred and ninety-one metres high) and to the south-east
the Karadağ chain (which is about one thousand, four
hundred and eighty-three metres high), while to the
north lies the mountain of Ulaştıran. Very near
to the castle is situated the spring of Karapinar, its
chalky waters forming calcified cascades as it falls from
the narrow gorge about one hundred metres to the
plain below where it joins the Alaca stream. In prehistoric times the flowing water of this stream had grad-
ually opened big holes in the soft earth of the mountain side, and later these became large caves. The scenery from here, as one looks towards the village of
Mustafa Çelebi, is very beautiful.

Since the castle is situated on the slopes of a hill where it is not very easy for earth to accumulate, and since the ground has also been constantly worked by the plough, the walls suffered a great deal of damage in consequence and many of the stones were displaced and rolled towards the edge of the hill.

An excavation was carried out in this area in (1937-1938) under the direction of Dr. Hamit Zübeyr Koşay, with the assistance of Mahmut Akok, Abdullah Altar, photographer Baha and others, on behalf of the Historical Association of Turkey.

Although Pazarlı is some way from the main transport routes and is slightly out of the way, nevertheless it is a suitable place to live in and easily defended and from the time of the Calcholithic age onwards (approximately 3500-3000 B.C.) the people of the plains have lived here, practising agriculture in clearings opened in the forests and turning it into a military outpost by means of its caves and natural fortifications which they turned into small castles.

At Pazarlı isolated remains of the Copper age and also of the Hittite age were found. The castle which one now sees belongs to the later Phrygian age (approximately 500 B.C.). During the excavations three architectural layers were discovered dating from the Phrygian age, but since the surface of the ground here is not at all smooth and is at the same time very sloping, besides the fact that it has suffered a great deal of damage, it has proved very difficult to establish the various layers.

The stone foundations and the entrance to the Phrygian courtyard are very distinctly seen, and the places where the turrets of the castle stood have been reinforced with heavy wood and stones. Inside the castle here and there various foundations of buildings may be seen, and amongst these, on the floor of one of the buildings on the southeastern side, a baked earthen frame and a mosaic made of painted nails have been discovered. It is thought that the upper parts of the castle ramparts have been given additional height by the construction of brick walls. It seems highly likely that some of the buildings were of two storeys since in some cases the remains of stone stairs can still be seen. The Phrygians were specially good in woodwork.

One of the houses, which belonged to a nobleman, possessed wooden panelling and outside carried pictures in relief and was covered with painted tiles. In these pictures which depict fighting animals (lion, bull, deer), two mountain goats standing on their hindlegs beside a tree, winged griffons, centaurs, parading soldiers with shields and spears, etc. are seen. Amongst the various different architectural devices which are used for the purpose of decoration on the exterior of the building painted geometric designs play a very great part.

Naturally both inside and in the vicinity of these buildings a number of objects in use among the Phrygians were discovered, as for instance pots, pans, metal instruments, etc. The most important of the finds from this site have been taken to the Ankara Museum (some cover-plates adorn the corridors of the Ankara Faculty of Languages, History and Geography), and a display was also arranged at the Alacahöyük local museum, those objects which are important for scientific study having been arranged and left at the Höyük museum depot.

The excavation group opened one of the tumuli at Pazarlı which had, however, been previously plundered and which belongs to the Hellenistic period. On the outskirts of Pazarlı and in its surrounding vicinity Hellenistic, Roman and Byzantine remains can all be seen.

Bibliography

Dr. Hamit Zübeyr Koşay : *Les Fouilles de Pazarlı*. Istanbul 1938. (This was delivered at the International Congress of History in Zurich, on the 4th of September, 1938).

Dr. Hamit Zübeyr Koşay : The report published by the Historical Congress of Turkey on the excavations at Pazarlı. Ankara 1941.

THE EXCAVATIONS OF BÜYÜK GÖLLÜCEK

Büyük Göllücek:

Büyük Göllücek is a village some fifteen kilometres to the north of Alacahöyük containing about sixty houses, and it is about fifteen minutes walk to the west of this village, at Kaletepe, that the Historical Association of Turkey carried out an excavation under the direction of Dr. Hamit Zübeyr Koşay and archaeologist Mahmut Akok in the years 1947 and 1949. Professor Muzaffer Şanyürek and archaeologist Raci Temizer joined the excavations in 1949. Kaletepe is situated in a chalky area about fifty metres above the Kale river and is surrounded with oak and pine trees.

The diameter of the mound on Kalatepe is about fifty metres and on it there are two damaged architectural layers of Phrygian origin, with beneath these two further, Calcholithic, layers. The importance of this excavation area is that here remains from the culture of the period 3500-3000 B.C. were found not only at surface level but on dry ground, as compared with the exceedingly difficult conditions prevailing at Alacahöyük. This was a cultural age when flints, obsidien and bone objects were all used at the same time. Only copper instruments were found in the whole excavation. Ninety-five percent of the objects found here consist of handmade pottery, and the prevailing colours are black, varying shades of red, brown, dirty yellow and greyish brown. One seldom meets thick lines of red and white decorations painted onto black surfaces. Some of the pots are angular in shape, and their handles are very primitive in design and shaped very close to the pots. Sometimes an excrescence shaped like a knob or double knob is used as a handle and on some very rare pots there is a knob actually on the handle. Sometimes this knob is in the form of an animal's head. There are also primitive examples of plates in the form of fruit plates. Only one skeleton was found from the Calcholithic age.

The square building in the lower area belonged to the Phrygians and some remnants of Phrygian settlements and even fortifications were found towards the northern slopes of Kaletepe towards the Akcaviran river.

Bibliography

Dr. Hamit Koşay   *First report on the researches* at Göllücek.
and Mahmut Akok: (*Belleten* XII, No 4, 46, 71-85 ; in Turkish and English).

Winifred Lamb   : *New Developments in Early Anatolian Archaeology.* 195-197 (The Discoveries at Göllücek).

Raci Temize.·   : *Kalınkaya Tümülüsü kazısı.* 1949 (*Belleten* vol. XIII No 52).
                    (This contains information on the Hellenistic tumulus excavated by the group, and also gives information on Gerdekkaya, Örükkaya).

BOĞAZKÖY

(Hattusas)

Although Alacahöyük was inhabited long before Boğazkale it can easily be surmised that at the time when Boğazkale was the capital of the Hittite Empire Alacahöyük was no more than a subsidiary of it, and its fortunes and actions were very much tied up with and governed by those of Boğazkale.

The History of the Excavations:

Boğazköy was discovered for the first time by Ch. Texier in 1834, following which G. Perrot in 1862 and E. Chantre in 1893-94 opened the way for the later excavations. When E. Chantre on the 17th of August 1894 at a meeting of the "Academie des Inscriptions et Belles-Lettres" introduced the cuneiform tablets which had been found here the world of scholarship proceeded to turn its attention to Central Asia, and the Germans, under the supervision and direction of H. Winckler, started to excavate in 1906-1907 with the co-operation of Makridi Bey, on behalf of the Müzei Hümayun (Royal Museum of Istanbul). They were later joined by O. Puchstein and the excavations continued in 1909-12. Writing in "Mitteilungen der Deutschen Orient Gesellschaft" (1907) H. Winckler put forth the view that Boğazköy was Chatti, the capital of the new Hittite Empire, and O. Puchstein, writing in

"Archeaologische Anzeiger" (1909) and in collabora-
tion with H. Kohl and D. Krenker in their book "Bo-
ğazköi I. Die Bau Werke" (1912) introduced to the le-
arned world all the architectural works which had been
found in Boğazköy. The Czechoslovakian scholar B.
Hrozny was successful in discovering the key to the
Hittite language and also found out the names of the
nineteen kings who reigned between the years 1600-
1200 B.C. (Hrozny: Bogazköi Studien 5./1920). These discoveries threw a great deal of light onto both Hittite history and cultural history, but since the first excavators gave prime importance to architecture and
epigraphy the result was that the stratigraphy of Boğazköy continued to remain in the dark. This was so
much the case that the small finds made there in the
meantime were not published until K. Bittel[1] wrote of
them (K. Bittel "Boğazköy, Die Klein Funde der Bra-
bungen" 1906-12/Leipzig 1937).

After the first World War the German Archaeological Institute started to excavate in this area of the
above mentioned Professor Kurt Bittel. In this excavation the work was concentrated on the main cita-
del - the Great Castle. In the former excavation over
8000 cuneiform tablets had been found and in the years 1931-33 a further 4700 tablets were discovered in
the building which housed the archives, amongst them
being royal seals, texts in Hittite, Protohittite, Babylo-
nian, Akkadian, and Akkadian-Sumerian dictionaries.
The texts contained valuable information concerning
religion, ceremony, mythology, and also in some parts
concerning history. The expedition carried out further

---

[1]   Professor K. Bittel is at present professor in the
Faculty of Letters, University of Istanbul.

excavations in the Hittite temple of Yazılıkaya, which is situated to the west of the Great Temple, as in the lower plain where the private houses were situated, and exact copies of the Yazılıkaya reliefs were made. However with the coming of the second World War the excavations came to an end. This excavation, in which a great many scholars took part, threw valuable light not only on the history of Boğazköy itself but also on the history of the whole of the Near East.

The following are some important works on the history of the excavations and the finds at Boğazköy:

Bibliography

K. Bittel : Mitt. Deutsch. Or. Ges. (M. D. O. G.) No. 70 (1932), No. 72 (1933), No. 77 (1939) introduced the first results here.

K. Bittel - H. G. Güterbock : Boğazköy, Neue Untersuchungen in der hethitischen Hauptstadt. Abh. Berlin 1935.

K. Bittel : Die Ruinen von Boğazköy, Der Hauptstadt des Hethiterreiches. Kurze Beschreibung. Berlin - Leipzig 1937 (in the form of a guide - book).

K. Bittel - R. Naumann : Boğazköy II. Neue Untersuchungen hethitischer Architektur. Abh. Berlin 1938 (introduces us to its architecture).

BOĞAZKÖY

Boğazköy is situated at an altitude of 940 metres, but at its southern end, which is called Yerkapı, its height reaches as much as 1240 metres. A small stream flows through the upper part of the town in the north and also through the lower part in the south. The whole town is surrounded with thick walls which are built on an earthen rampart, and also by a number of moats. Six hillocks within the town itself and one hillock outside the town were fortified, and inside the Great City Walls the town was divided up into various sections, in just the same manner as it was in Zincirli and Ekbatana. Büyükkale (The Great Castle) was the place where the government administration offices and the archives were centred and this part is 1228 metres high. At Yerkapı there is a tunnel some seventy metres in length, opening off which is the door with the Sphinxes; to the east lies the Royal gate and the Lion's Gate, while by the side of the stream yet another gate is situated. In the upper town four temples have been discovered, and in the lower town lies a temple which covers an area of 64 x 42 metres. Besides the Great Temple there are stores and various other buildings, and in some of these stores a great number of tablets were discovered. The frieze which was found over the Royal Gate, mentioned above, represents a god and this has been removed to the Ankara Museum.

Cultural layers of Boğazköy:

Up to the present date five cultural layers (1-V) have been established at Boğazköy.

Layer V:

This is the lowest level, and has been dated in a limited area by the Cappadocian ceramics (XIXth to XXth century B.C.) and at Büyükkale with the Alişar I ceramics (2500 B.C.). K. Bittel basing his results on the tablets says that the layer where the Cappadocian ceramics were found belonged to the period of King Piusti, the local king, who was later destroyed by the Kussar King Anita.

Layer IV:

(The layers c, b, a,) The Old Empire Age: At layer IVc were discovered the grey ceramics which were also met with at Ahlatlibel, Alişar and in Persia (although the New Bronze types resemble those of the Minoan age they are in reality older).

In layers b and a, like those in Alişar II, we find red painted, shiny ceramics. It is definitely known that Hattusas was established as the capital in the time of the Hittite kings Bitkhana and Anita. In the age of Dudhalias III (the father of Shubbiluliuma), at the end of the XVth century B.C. Boğazköy was burnt to the ground by the Gasgasians and after this commenced an age of decline, when most of the inhabitants left the town.

Layer III:

A and b.

A: The burnt city was again rebuilt. In this layer Shubbiluliuma's "bulla" was found. (Bittel: Neue Untersuhungen, pp. 14-15, 25, 27). The battle of Kadesh was fought in the year 1289 B.C. between Muvattalis and Rameses II. Layer IIIb dates from the period 1280-1200 B.C. By this time the emigration of the tribes from the northern and coastal areas had commenced. In the year 1225 B.C. the northern tribes were using Hittite buildings, and by 1200 B.C. they were strengthening the walls in Egypt.

Layer II:

The Phrygian age: After the Phrygian age the Anatolian plateau became divided between the Lydians and the Medes. This period is contemporary with Alişar V.

Yazılıkaya:

Is situated about two kilometres to the east of Boğazköy. It is a temple belonging to the period of the Hittite state. The chief gods and goddesses are shown in relief carved on rocks in the hierarchical manner and every god has its name written with hierogliphs. These reliefs are divided into two sections. In the larger of these divisions, which comprises the northern section, there is depicted a procession of the gods and goddesses, while in the smaller division is seen the procession of gods carrying weapons in the shape of scythes, with King Tuthaliya who is seen as being held in the arms of the god of thunder, Dadamimas, and receiving his protection. In front of these sections lie the temple foundations and the stairs. (Bittel-Naumann-Oto: **Yazilikaya**, 1941; Bittel: **Die Felsbilder von Yazilikaya 1934**).

The Treasures from the B. tomb. (Alacahöyük)

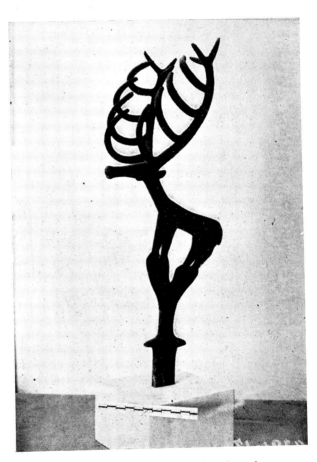

Adeer found in one of the Royal tombs

The door with the Sphinxes (Alacahöyük).

The foundations of a Hittite building at Alacahöyük

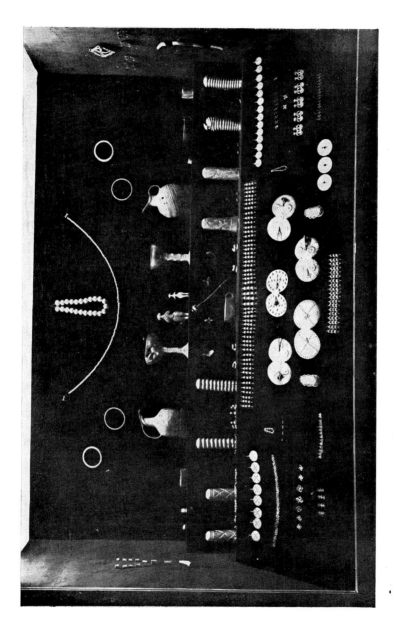

Some of the treasures found at Alacahöyük.

Yazılıkaya. Boğazkale.

The Temple of Yazılıkaya (A. section) Boğazkale

The foundations of a Hittite building at Alacahöyük

Some of the treasures found at Alacahöyük.

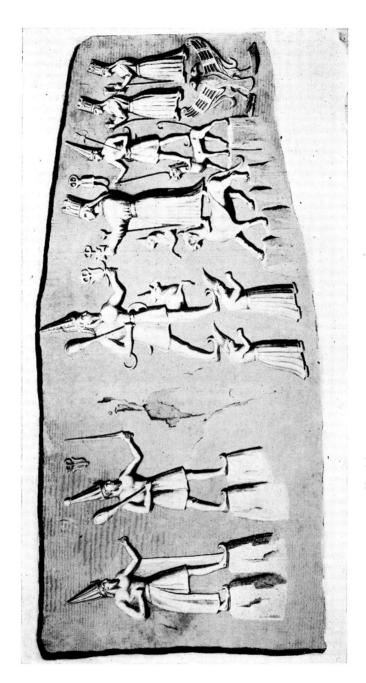

Yazılıkaya, a scene depicting the meeting or marriage of the Gods. Boğazkale

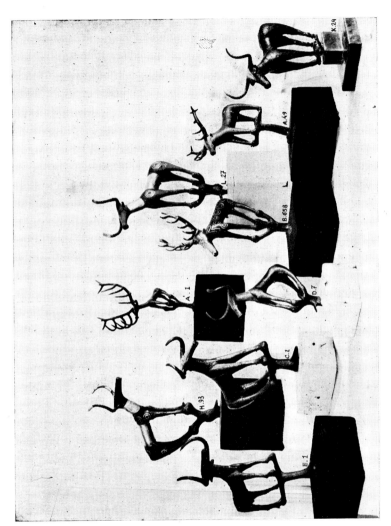

The deers found in the Royal tombs at Alacahöyük. (circa 2400 B.C)

Pazarlı.

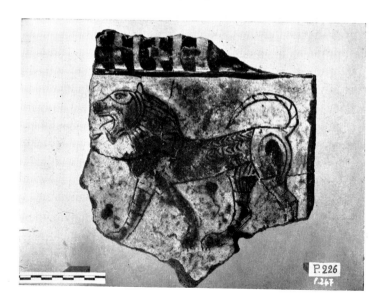

A wall painting found at Pazarlı ( ).

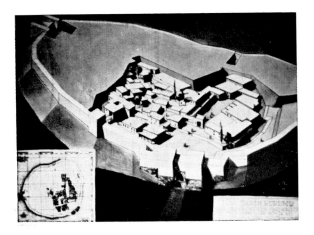

Alacahöyük at the time of the New (Hittite Empire.)

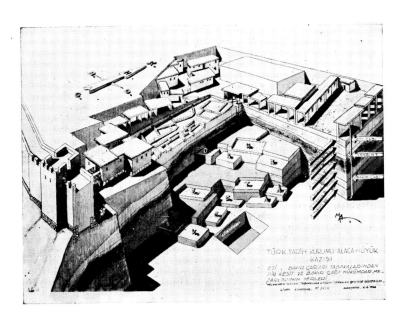

The position of the Royal tombs at Alacahöyük, also showing
the various layers.

The transportation of a huge Hittite jug.

A Hiitite larder and another huge jug

A phrygian releif, showing a centaur carrying a bush

A jar with two handles
(Büyük göllücek)

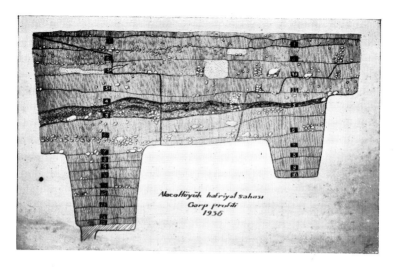

The West profile of the Alacahöyük, excavation area,
showing the various cultural layers

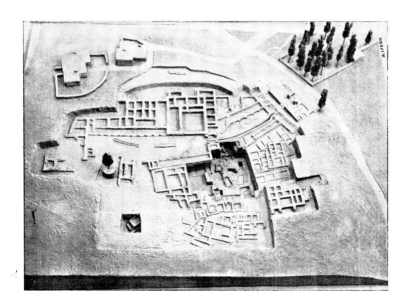

A general plan of Alacahöyük.

Örülü Kaya Roman acquaduct on the South of Alaca.

Alacahöyük.

A tomb at Alacahöyük

A Hittite water jug found at Alacahöyük.

The repairing of Hittite jugs found at Alacahöyük.

Specimens of Hittite pottery found at Alacahöyük.

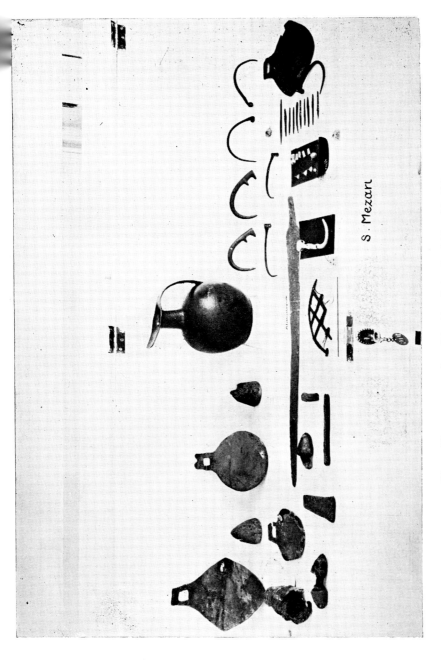

S. Mezarı

28 — The treasures found in the S tomb. (Alacahöyük).

L. Mezarı

The treasures found in the L tomb. (Alacahöyük).

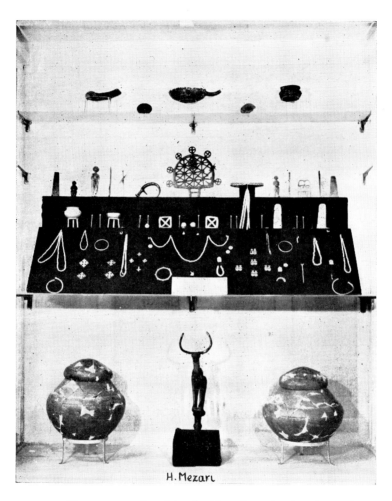

H. Mezarı

The treasures found in the H tomb. (Alacahöyük).

D. Mezarı

The treasures found in the D tomb. (Alacahöyük).

K. Mezarı

The treasures found in the K tomb. (Alacahöyük).

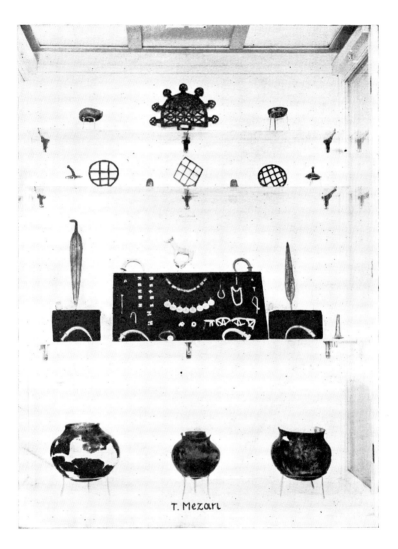

T. Mezarı

The treasures found in the T tomb. (Alacahöyük).

C. Mezarı

34 — The treasures found in the C tomb. (Alacahöyük).

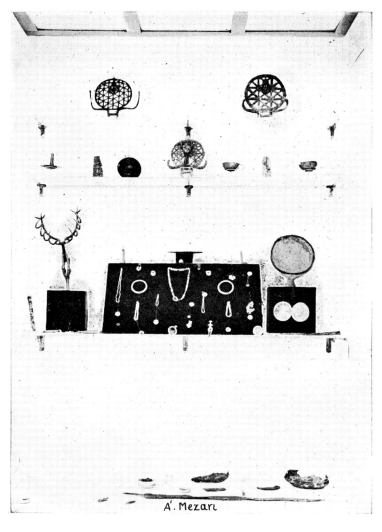

A'. Mezarı

The treasures found in the A tomb. (Alacahöyük).

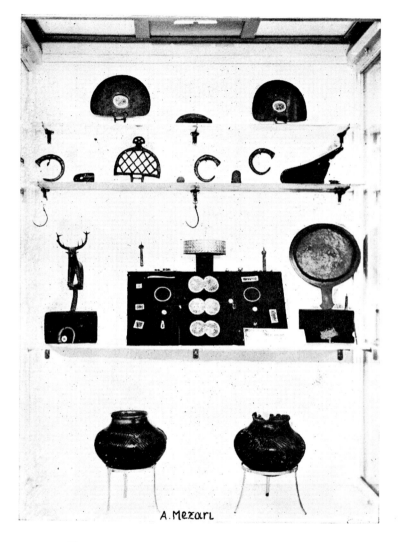

A. Mezarı

The treasuree found in the A tomb (Alacahöyük)

Phrygian pottery found at Pazarlı.

The excavation house musuem at alacahöyük

Upper part of a pot of the Phrygian period found in the District
of Pazarlı (Çıkhasan)

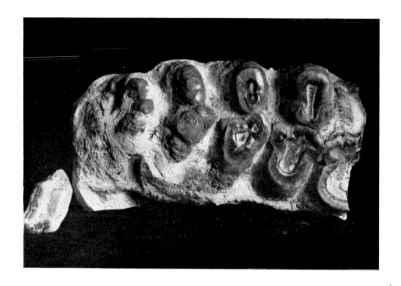

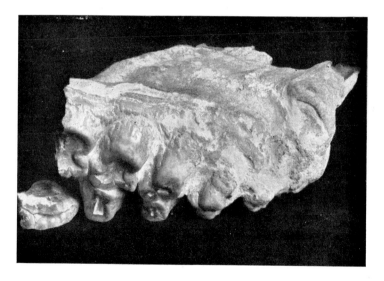

28 — A row of teeth belonging to an animal which lived in the prehistoric times. It was found while searching for pebbles on a terrace in the South of Alaca. The teeth belong to a Mastadon.

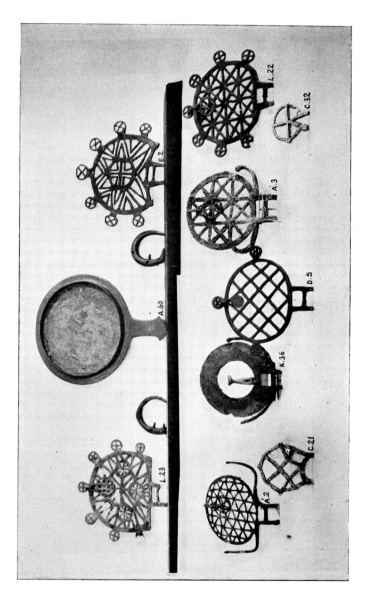

Various sun discs found in royal tombs of the old Bronze Age at
Alaca - Hüyük

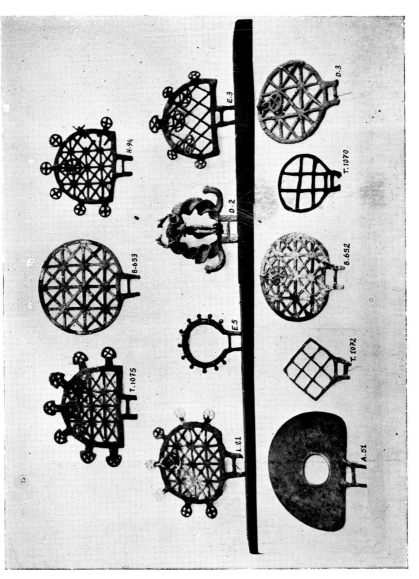

Various sun discs found in royal tombs of the old Bronze Age at
Alaca - Höyük